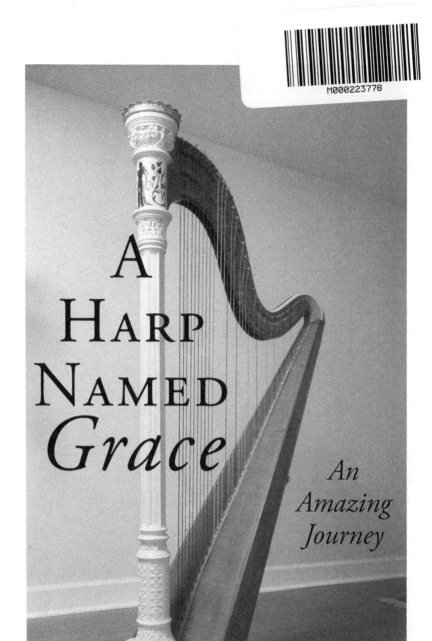

A HARP NAMED Grace

An Amazing Journey

Verlon Eason

ISBN 978-1-0980-6778-6 (paperback)
ISBN 978-1-0980-6779-3 (digital)

Copyright © 2020 by Verlon Eason

All rights reserved. No part of this publication may be reproduced, distributed, or transmitted in any form or by any means, including photocopying, recording, or other electronic or mechanical methods without the prior written permission of the publisher. For permission requests, solicit the publisher via the address below.

Christian Faith Publishing, Inc.
832 Park Avenue
Meadville, PA 16335
www.christianfaithpublishing.com

Printed in the United States of America

Dedication

This book is dedicated to all the beautiful souls I've been privileged to minister to on the harp and to all the people mentioned in this book who played a vital role encouraging me along my journey. Most importantly to my husband of 46 years and best friend, Doug, who tirelessly has been my harp hauler and quiet cheerleader always believing in me and encouraging me to believe in my dreams. And above all to my Lord Jesus Christ, whom without Him, none of this would have ever happened.

Soli Deo Gloria!

Thank you,

Verlon Eason
March 30, 2020

Note: Since the publishing process began of this book, both Verlon's sister and dad passed away three months apart. They played a special part in her story and will be deeply missed.

FOREWORD

Verlon Eason, the author of *A Harp Named Grace: An Amazing Journey*, is my beloved and humble friend whom I greatly admire. She has penned her journey in hopes that others will be inspired to use their God-given gifts as well. Yes, we all need encouragement on our personal journey through life.

At an incredibly young age, Verlon won multiple vocal awards and began piano lessons, later graduating from college with a BA degree in music. In a short period of time, she sadly lost several close family members. After fighting depression, she realized that God was with her through life's storms, and she sensed He had a plan to bring her through this difficult time. A very unexpected Christmas gift helped steer her on a meaningful journey that would blossom into a never-ending service to others.

The message that burned into Verlon's heart found her researching and studying to craft her talent on several amazing instruments. Her thirst to learn and her desire to understand minute details have benefited countless students. They have been loved and encouraged by a patient teacher who knows her trade well.

My hat is off to Verlon's patient, loving, and supportive husband, Doug, who has moved her large costly harp to hundreds of engagements, loading and unloading it countless times to serve others. This dear man of God is truly *one* of a kind!

A Harp Named Grace has inspired me, and I believe it will inspire you and others as we proceed on our journey through life.

Shirley Balmer-Jordan
Christian/gospel pianist

PART 1

CHAPTER I

"I will praise you, O Lord, with all my heart; I will tell of all your wonders"

(Psalm 9:1).

Now as I think about it, the seed was planted in me as a young girl. I remember seeing one, thinking how beautiful it was. *Who could ever be so lucky to play one?* I thought. Never in a million years did I ever contemplate that I could be *that* lucky one someday! My mother saw to it that her daughters would have music in their lives. She whetted our appetites with everything musical—from tap dance, ballet, singing, and piano lessons. The latter two kept my attention, and I grew to love them both. I remember hearing Daddy singing a lot when he was home from his long traveling jobs. He was very talented working with his hands building things. He'd sing a lot as he worked on his favorite projects. I can still hear him today. He had a really nice voice, I thought. I soon learned to love singing also and began singing on stage at the young age of four. Mrs. Catherine Boswell was my personality voice teacher, and Momma told me she had great faith in me with my God-given potential. She put me in many talent competitions where I won a number of awards singing on stage before large crowds of people. Sadly, though, those years were short-lived when Mrs. Boswell died. I didn't study voice again till many years later. I took a real interest in playing the piano, which became a big focus of my life. I loved playing the piano and knew that would be my life's fulfillment. Then one day, Momma discovered another voice teacher who lived less than a mile from our new house in Atlanta.

A sweet lady she was, and there in her house stood *one*. That *beautiful, striking, exquisite instrument! Hmm, how nice*, I thought, *having one of them in your house!* How very lucky she was! Yes, I did take voice lessons from her as I continued studying piano, but never did it even cross my mind then that I could play one at that time in my life. *Only special people play the* harp, I thought. My parents loved to go "antiquing," as they called it. My sister and I didn't, so we got to stay home, and we were glad. Another day, after my daddy had come home from one of his long traveling jobs, I heard him singing again in the basement as he worked on his new project. He and Momma had bought *it* the last time they went antiquing. Actually later, I found out they exchanged something they owned for *it. Hmm, it looked pretty rough, though*, I thought. How would Daddy ever make something beautiful out of *that*? Time would show that he did, though. Daddy had that magic touch that he could take anything junky and turn it into something gorgeous. And he did too! I watched him as he tried to remove the thick white paint that covered this treasure. You could see the *gold* underneath it, and I remember thinking, *Why would anyone ever paint over that incredible gold?* There was even a gold crown that set on top, as if on a princess's head. Later I would know that piece to be known as a column that held the crown. In time, Daddy finished this amazing project, and he and Momma were so proud to set this antique treasure in our living room close to the piano I practiced on daily. Even though it was a beautiful piece to behold, you could still see parts of this instrument that needed major repair by someone who knew a lot about this instrument. Yet still I never even thought that one day I could play this musical treasure. I had only seen them in pictures or in movies perhaps but never had I ever seen someone playing *one* up close in person. No, we never went to hear the symphony where I was sure to see one being played there. It was only in my dreams that I could picture a beautiful lady with long flowing hair playing the most heavenly instrument I'd ever seen know as *the harp*!

Antique Harp Crown

CHAPTER 2

"To everything there is a season, a time for every purpose under heaven"

(Ecclesiastes 3:1).

I don't know why it never crossed my mind as a child to ask if I could learn to play the harp. I chalk it up to the fact that it just wasn't God's timing. You know how the Bible says, "To everything there is a season." Well, I guess my "season" hadn't come. God had that special time and place that the harp would fit into His perfect plan for my life.

Many years had passed after my first close encounter with the harp my parents owned. Since music had played a big part of my life and brought me much fulfillment, it was natural that I would go to college and major in music. I studied piano vocal music education at the University of South Florida and graduated with a BA degree. A year later, I met my husband, Doug. We got married and began raising our two fine sons. All the while, I taught private music lessons and was quite involved in many musical activities. I always knew God had given me a special musical talent, and I freely used my gifts to serve Him wherever He led me. However, after a long period of time, I began to feel burnout infiltrating me, and I attempted to find as many ways I could to ignite a new fire within me, but nothing seemed to satisfy me. Boredom filled me, and I prayed for new revitalization, but I didn't know how or when it would happen. Looking back on that season of my life, I realize it was all a part of God's plan. Even though the spark had dimmed over those years, I kept teaching, trying to be faithful in using the talent God had entrusted to me.

Then one day, a whole new set of circumstances occurred that would turn out to change the course of my life forever.

Dad, as I called him (even though he was my father-in-law), was like a dear father to me. Being the wife of his firstborn son, Dad and I had a special bond. Johnny was a dear soul and was loved by everyone who knew him. He was a hardworking man who loved the Lord and his family with all his heart. It was discovered that he had a tumor that required surgery. Pre-op tests revealed that he needed open-heart surgery before having the tumor removed. During the Christmas season of 1990, open-heart surgery was performed. The health care professional told us the risk of stroke following this type of surgery and every precaution would be observed. Unfortunately, the hospital was understaffed during the holidays, and Dad didn't receive the care he needed. We called Dad Christmas morning to wish him Merry Christmas and tell him we would visit him soon. Upon answering the telephone, he didn't know who we were. Panic filled our hearts, and we quickly rushed to the hospital. It was evident Dad had suffered a stroke and soon had to be transported to another hospital specializing in treatment of stroke patients. After many months of rehab, Dad was finally released to go home. What a happy day that was! Now all that Dad needed were a lot of rest and relaxation to prepare for the tumor surgery.

Early February was the determined date for his surgery. With much prayer, we knew Dad was in God's hands. Dad was a strong healthy man who seemed to never get sick, and we felt he would come through the surgery just fine. The surgery was performed, and the diagnosis was not what we expected to hear. The tumor was malignant, and cancer had spread throughout his body. We were told he didn't have long to live. Time with Dad at the hospital in the days that followed held precious memories we would always remember. How does one say goodbye to one soul so dear? With our faith in God, we knew Dad was in His merciful hands and all would be okay. Family members came to say their goodbyes to Dad, and within a few days, he was ushered into the arms of his Lord and Savior, Jesus Christ.

CHAPTER 3

It wasn't long until I phoned my parents to tell them the news of Johnny's passing. They dearly loved Johnny and had a close relationship with him and his wife, Betty. Mom and Dad, as I called them, always made my folks feel at home when they visited and enjoyed one another's company a lot. Naturally, my folks wanted to attend the funeral.

When I called my parents, Daddy said Mamma wasn't feeling well, but she still wanted to make the eight-hour drive from Georgia. My sister, Jayne, a nurse, rode down with them; and upon their arrival, I could tell my mom didn't feel well by her demeanor. In her petite frame of four feet and eleven and a half inches, Mamma looked frail and weak and certainly not herself. I was very concerned for her well-being. I knew she belonged back home under her doctor's care; but trying to help my mother-in-law, Betty, with funeral arrangements kept my mind occupied for the next few days.

Just as we imagined, many people attended Johnny's service. He had been a tractor salesman for many years, winning numerous company awards for outstanding sales. Dad was loved by many and rich in friendships. There was no doubt about that by seeing all the people who attended his service.

My family decided to stay in a nearby motel following the funeral and spoke briefly about staying a few extra days at the beach before traveling home to Atlanta, but instincts told me they needed to get Momma back home to the doctor. Early the next morning, Daddy called and said they were leaving for home soon with plans to meet Momma's doctor at the hospital. I asked if they would stop by our house before leaving town, but Daddy said he felt he needed to get her home as soon as possible. Suddenly a voice quickened within me telling me to hurry and see them before they left town. I hopped in my car and took off in a hurry, praying as hard as I could.

Upon entering the motel room, Momma was lying on the bed, looking dreadful. In my distress, I gazed over at her, and she said, "Verlon, I'm dying." I cried and reassured her she was going to be okay and that Daddy and my sister were going to see that she got the care she needed. I reminded her that God was with her, taking care of her. In my sobs, I affirmed our love and God's strong love for her. Peering down at her frail little legs in their darkened state, I commented to my sister how horrible they appeared. She echoed her concern to me as well.

Soon they were ready to leave for home, and before pulling out, Daddy said they would call me as soon as they arrived at the hospital. Waving my goodbyes with a heavy heart, I drove home to my house in Casselberry, Florida.

Daddy's Music Stand that he built

CHAPTER 4

All day long, the hours seemed to drag, and I couldn't help feeling anxious and stressed about Momma's health. Cell phones were not prevalent at that time, so we lacked the convenience of making frequent calls to check up on Momma's condition.

Our sons, Ryan and Robby, were in school; and later that afternoon, they had a little league baseball game. With the game lasting several hours, I knew we would not return home till around 7:00 p.m. There was dinner to prepare, and I knew my husband, Doug, wouldn't get home from work till about 7:30 that evening.

Because I was so worried about Momma's health, I called her doctor's office earlier that day asking them to please call me as soon as they knew Momma's diagnosis. They assured me they would. My folks thought very highly of their doctor and had complete confidence in him. It was only later that I discovered the doctor strongly disagreed that Momma should leave Orlando when he realized her worsened condition when they arrived in town. The doctor strongly suggested she be taken to a hospital in Orlando rather than attempt the long trip home with her feeling so ill. Still, Daddy had a lot of confidence in the doctor and wanted him to examine her himself. Therefore, they made the trip that day, expecting to arrive in Atlanta late that afternoon with plans of meeting the doctor at the hospital.

Early afternoon, Daddy stopped to fill up the car with gas. Momma, sitting in the front seat of their red Cadillac, mentioned to Daddy that her leg hurt. Daddy suggested she lay her head back and try to rest, knowing they would be home in a couple of hours.

After driving on the interstate for a while, Daddy noticed Momma was leaning next to her door while sleeping and mentioned to Jayne to prop her up with a pillow for comfort. Jayne was reaching out to prop Momma up when instantly she knew some-thing was wrong. Momma's body felt cold! In panic, Jayne cried out, "Daddy, she's dead!" Quickly, Daddy pulled off the interstate to check her, and sure enough, she had peacefully passed away soon after closing her eyes for a nap. With tears and heavy hearts, they made their three-hour trip home with Momma dead in the front seat of their car.

CHAPTER 5

Daddy drove straight to the hospital where the doctor informed them that the pain in Momma's leg was due to a blood clot that traveled to her heart, which eventually took her life. One thing we were so thankful for was that she didn't suffer and died peacefully.

Taking my sons to their baseball practice that afternoon gave my mind a reprieve from worry about Momma's condition. After returning home, I knew I would soon get a phone call from Daddy telling me how Momma was doing. It was 7:30 p.m. that Tuesday, February 11, 1992, when the call came from Daddy. His voice sounded calm yet strong when he asked if Doug was home from work yet. I replied no but was sure he would be walking in the door any minute. I asked Daddy how Momma was doing and what the doctor's diagnosis was. His voice broke; and after a long pause, he said, "Honey, I didn't want to tell you until Doug got home, but your Momma is gone. She died in the car on our way home." In complete shock and hysteria, I fell apart in tears. Just then, Doug came walking in the door. God knew just how much I needed to see him and be held by my husband at that exact moment! All I remember is that I couldn't stop crying. I felt like my life had been turned completely upside down.

The hours that followed seemed somewhat vivid with some dear friends coming to our home to offer their condolences and help. Our pastor, Rev. Ken Crossman and his wife, Cecily, visited us, offering words of comfort and love. He then spoke some words directly to me that I shall never forget—words that would later prove to be quite prophetic. He said, "Verlon, you must let her go." Those words seemed to echo in my mind repeatedly. I remember thinking how in the world I could let go of the one who gave me life and whom I loved so much! As God would later reveal to me, I knew my pastor's words would forever be imprinted in my mind and on my heart.

Early the next morning the phone began ringing with calls from close friends, offering words of peace, comfort, and a multitude of prayers. Many people in our church family brought prepared food which was so appreciated. One dear friend, Barbara Shady, offered to take me shopping for clothes to wear to the funeral. Another very close sister in Christ, Sandy Galarza, sacrificed many hours to comfort me by staying overnight and reading scriptures about heaven and reminding me that Momma was no longer in pain. She was, indeed, walking the streets of gold, swimming in the River of Life spoken in the book of Revelation and being reunited with loved ones gone before her. Most importantly, though, she was seeing her Lord and Savior Jesus Christ!

Words from the scriptures brought me so much comfort to my soul, enabling me to rest peacefully through the night. Looking back on that time, God had truly sent ministering angels to bring peace to my heart through the rough storm I was walking through. Losing two parents in the same week was more than I could bear; yet somehow, deep inside, I knew God would grant me the strength I so desperately needed to get through this tough time in my life.

My First Lever Harp given by my Dad

CHAPTER 6

"I waited patiently for the Lord; He turned to me and heard my cry. He lifted me out of the slimy pit, out of the mud and mire. He set my feet on a rock, making my footsteps firm. And He put a new song in my mouth, a song of praise to our God" (Psalm 40:1–3).

> "Why are you in despair, O my soul? Hope in God, for I shall again praise Him for the help of His presence" (Psalm 42:5).

The weeks that followed the death of my mother and father-in-law left me completely drained. I felt like I was sinking into a deep pit and needed a hand to pull me out. Yet at the same time, strangely as it seemed, feelings of anger seemed to well up within me. I was crying out to God, "Why, oh, why did this have to happen!" Two family members whom I loved so dearly both taken away just days apart! My heart felt so wounded, and I needed to understand *why* God had brought me to this place of deep pain. Was this a test to build my character or to help me learn to trust God in the midst of all circumstances?

Yes, Christ had been my Lord and Savior for a long time, and reading the Bible taught me that as Christians we all go through sufferings in this life. No one is exempt from pain. As I later came to realize, "Yes" was the answer to my questions. As the Lord reminded me, "*When* you pass through the waters, I will be with you. And through the rivers, they will not overflow you. *When* you walk through the fire, you will not be scorched, nor will the flame burn you. For I am the Lord your God" (Isaiah 43:2). Indeed, God was saying He was in control and I was not alone. He was with me and would help me through this storm. He also revealed to me in my quiet times with Him that He was loving on me even in my most broken places, that He hurt with me but He had a plan for me so much higher than I could ever imagine. He had a plan to bring *good* out of all my hurt and pain (Romans 8:28)! Despite the depression I found myself in, God was filling me with hope every time I turned to Him instead of choosing not to wallow in self-pity. Again and again, He was faithful to remind me of all His wonderful promises, and that included one of my favorite scriptural promises: "For I know the plans I have for you, declared the Lord, plans for good and not for evil, to give you a future and a hope" (Jeremiah 29:11).

Yes, surely He knew the plans He had for my life—plans to complete me. Now my part was to trust Him as I waited upon Him.

CHAPTER 7

"For out of the abundance of the heart, the mouth speaks"

(Matthew 12:34b).

Daddy and I talked by phone frequently now that Momma was gone. I wanted to check up on him regularly since we lived about five hundred miles apart. Knowing his daughter well, he was concerned as much for me as I was for him. We expressed our deep sadness and feelings of despair which we knew was all a part of the grieving process. Somehow, though, we knew it was helpful for both of us to talk openly about our feelings and the pain we felt.

One day, Daddy asked me a question that would prove to be life changing: "Honey, is there anything that would make you feel better?" Out of the blue, when I opened my mouth to speak, these words came: *"I want to play a harp!"*

After I spoke these seemingly magical words, I couldn't believe what I said! Where did these words come from? I had not even thought of this before! What was this all about? Later, God would reveal He was the One who put it in my spirit! We talked about where we could find a harp, and we remembered having seen some folk harps in a historic village not far from my dad's home in Atlanta. He began researching, and we left the subject dormant for a while.

Christmas was soon approaching, and Daddy decided to come to Florida to spend the holidays with us. Before gathering his personal belongings from his car, first, he lifted a *very* large box, and he had the biggest grin I had ever seen on his face! We all smiled as he brought it into the house and set it near the Christmas tree, saying, "Hmm, I wonder what *this* could be and *who* this is for!" My heart skipped several beats, and like a kid, I couldn't wait for Christmas to arrive the next day!

I opened the large box the next morning with a smile from ear to ear on my face, and uncovering this mysterious item proved to be exactly what God had laid upon my heart…a *harp*! Oh my! A harp just for *me*? My mind quickly recalled my childhood memories thinking that "only angels play the harp"! Within seconds of thinking that, a still small voice spoke to me, saying, "Yes, that's right. You, my child, are *my angel* that I'm calling to play this special instrument." Suddenly, a peace flooded my heart that told me God had spoken prophetic words to my spirit. Somehow, I knew in my heart at that moment that he had a brand-new plan for my life and I would never be the same person again. A new change, a new hope, a strange new beginning! All of a sudden, I was so excited about what the future held for me, and I couldn't wait for His perfect plan to unfold!

Salvi Eire Lap Harp "GRACIE"

CHAPTER 8

"I will sing a new song to You, O God; on a harp
of ten strings I will sing praise to You"

(Psalm 144:9).

Having received my new harp as a gift from my dad, I couldn't
wait to start playing it. Yes, I knew it was definitely different from
playing the piano, but in my mind's eye, I figured it had to be somewhat similar since they were both technically stringed instruments.
I had a BA degree in piano, and I hoped that gave me some knowledge I needed to play the harp well. I thought, *How hard could it
really be?* even though I always heard it was one of *the* most difficult
instruments to ever play! Daddy had given me a "how-to" book on
playing the harp, and I figured it couldn't be *that* hard, so I proceeded to teach myself...kinda like following an instruction manual.
(Ha, what a joke, I would later discover!) After soon completing the
book, I was quite pleased that I had taught myself so quickly (and
I thought, pretty well). Ha! God quickly showed me that He had a
keen sense of humor by allowing me to think I could learn to play
the harp on my own without any assistance of a trained instructor.
Besides, in all my years of teaching piano and belonging to music
clubs and organizations, never had I encountered a harp instructor. I
thought what an arduous task that would surely be—to find a harp
teacher in the same town where I lived. Never had it entered my
mind to *pray* for a teacher. How quickly I had forgotten that *God*
was the *one who* gave me the harp, and if He supplied that, surely He
would provide the right instructor who would teach me the correct
and necessary skills to play well.

After having received my first harp Christmas 1993, I was excited to tell others about my new endeavor. In January 1994, I had a dental appointment; and while my dentist was examining my teeth (and of course, I couldn't speak with his hands in my mouth!), he shared with me about a wonderful Christmas party he had attended during the holidays and that this lady had a "room *full of harps!*" When he said that, my eyes broadened; and I began gagging, wanting to ask him who this lady was. I said, "You said she had a room full of harps?" "Yes," he proclaimed. I quickly asked him if he would give me her name, and he replied, "Of course." Upon leaving the office, I found myself mesmerized about the conversation I just had with my dentist, of all people, talking about the instrument I had quickly fallen in love with. With a skip in my step, I left the dentist office and couldn't wait to get home to call this new harp instructor and see if she was available to begin teaching me.

The phone rang, and a professional voice answered, "This is harpist, Jan Jennings. May I help you?" "Yes," I replied, "you may." I told her about the conversation I had with Dr. Diefenderfer and discovered he was her dentist as well. I inquired about harp lessons and told her of my musical background. She asked if I owned a harp, of which I replied, "Yes." Then she inquired what type of harp I owned. I proudly told her that my dad had it made for me. She invited me to come hear her play at a Sunday brunch before attending my first lesson. Upon telling my husband, I couldn't wait for Sunday to come so that I could really hear someone proficiently and professionally play the most wonderful instrument in the world!

CHAPTER 9

What an absolute joy it was to see someone up close playing her harp and truly enjoying it. She played with such grace and proficiency that it made me want to begin lessons with her that very day. Well, the day of my first real harp lesson finally came, and I was so excited to learn all about this fabulous instrument.

My instructor explained all the necessary skills to play the harp *well*... Thumbs up! I rehearsed this in my mind constantly and continued to go regularly to my lessons. After a number of months, I had acquired quite a few harp CDs, and listening to them inspired me to keep persevering till I could play the harp well. As all harpists know, this is not an instrument you learn overnight but rather requires hours and hours of practice. Not just practice but *correct* practice! Thumbs up, close the thumb, fingers in the palm, open and close, etc.! Even though I had a music degree in piano, I soon realized that the harp was not even closely related, due to the specialized technic. Over time, I did hear of self-taught harpers and saw some play, but I soon realized the importance of playing well being linked to having a good harp instructor. I was very thankful God had blessed me with a good teacher.

It wasn't long before I soon realized that the harp my dad gifted me with was not going to take me where I wanted to go in playing the harp. I wanted to be a serious harpist and play the very best I possibly could. Indeed, I was extremely thankful for the harp my dad had given me. It was truly a "heart gift" from my earthly father, handed down from my "heavenly Father." My first harp had truly been used over a period of time to heal my broken heart in the death of my dear momma and father-in-law, and for that, I would forever be grateful. The Lord had done amazing things using the harp as a healing tool in my life.

As I played the harp, the vibrations of the strings with the instrument lying close to my heart brought a special peace to my soul, a peace unlike anything else I had ever experienced before. Over time, I could tell I felt different inside. My moods changed, and I had a deeper abiding peace that lingered with me as I played. It was surreal! I loved playing the harp and the peace and joy it brought to my heart and soul transcended anything I had ever experienced in my entire life.

I often thought about David, the shepherd boy from the Psalms in the Bible who played his harp while tending his sheep, and the many songs he wrote while worshiping the Lord. I remembered how David was asked to play his harp for King Saul, who suffered from depression, and how the soothing harp sounds ministered to the king's spirit (1 Samuel 16:12–23). God frequently reminded me of the healing powers of the harp and soon revealed it to my spirit that the harp, indeed, was being used to heal my broken heart in the loss of my loved ones. *How amazing*, I thought! My mind was completely being renewed about the amazing affects the harp had upon people. I had also observed the calming affects playing the harp had upon my dog. It was definitely special and unlike any other instrument I had ever encountered. As I began to ponder on the therapeutic affects the harp had on me, I thought surely it could be used to touch and bring healing to other people as well.

Kennor (Psalmist David's harp)

CHAPTER 10

"And my God shall supply all your needs according to His riches in glory in Christ Jesus"
(Philippians 4:19).

After studying harp for a period of time with my instructor, I knew I would need a full-size pedal harp so I would progress well and accelerate my learning skills. Although I had rented a semigrand pedal harp for some time now, I knew I needed to own one myself, but the expense of purchasing one kept me from moving forward.

My husband and I were in the middle of building our dream home. And our assets were tied up in the house. Still, deep down inside my heart, I sensed the Lord wanted me to believe that I could own my own pedal harp. He reminded me of James 1:5, "If any of you lack wisdom, let him ask of God, who gives to all men generously and without reproach, and it will be given to him, but let him ask in faith without any doubting." And then Matthew 7:5 came to me, "Ask and it shall be given to you, seek and you shall find; knock and the door shall be opened to you." I prayed faithfully and waited patiently for Him to open the door in His perfect timing. I told the Lord that if He would grant me my own pedal harp, I wanted to name her Grace because it would be His amazing *grace* that would give her to me. Well, God surely heard my heart, and then the door opened wide!

My harp instructor told me about a lady who lived in the Orlando area who wanted to sell her semigrand Lyon & Healy pedal harp. Curiously, I decided to go check it out. Upon arriving at her lovely home, I soon discovered there were several other interested buyers there as well. Being the "third" interested customer, I had doubts that I would be able to purchase it. After all, it was a *lot* of money, and besides I was third in line. Even if this was "the one," no doubt I would need a miracle!

As I began talking with the owner after the other people left, I learned her name was Mrs. Cross and that her deceased husband had been a pastor. *Hmm, what a unique name for a pastor's wife!* I thought. She was a kind, gentle soul, and our spirits connected immediately. She asked me if I'd like to play her harp. "Absolutely," I replied. After playing a few pieces, she kindly looked at me and said, "Verlon, God wants *you* to have this harp!" My heart sank, and I felt elated with joy and still humbled with gratitude for His goodness! We talked at length, and the comradery we shared was priceless. I told her I was waiting for a financial miracle if God wanted me to buy her harp which she understood. Upon leaving her home, I asked Mrs. Cross, "By the way, did you ever name your harp?" She replied, "Of course, I named her Grace!" I knew that was a divine sign that He was going to make a way for me to own her!

I soon hurried home and told my husband about this amazing discovery, and immediately we both knew God would make a way for us to purchase Grace. As it turned out, doors closed for the other people interested in the harp, but God opened the door wide for us to own Grace, and she proudly became my own. Within a year after owning her, doors amazingly opened for opportunities to perform in ministry, and every dollar was returned to its needed place. What a mighty God we serve!

CHAPTER 11

A year or more after I became the happy new owner of Grace, I attended a harp conference and was supposed to have my dear harpist friend, Vicki Garcia, as my roommate. Unfortunately, she was unable to attend, and I had a hotel room all to myself for the entire weekend. Somehow I felt like God planned it that way for a reason. Even though I missed my friend, I knew the alone time was somehow meant to be.

I had begun this new exciting journey learning to play my harp and felt God had a special plan for me ever since I started playing. I had not a clue what He had in store, but I felt a great anticipation of what the future held for me and Grace.

One evening while reading my Bible in my hotel room, I felt God speak to me about a plan He had for me. I heard Him speak to my spirit with these words: "Verlon, I want to use you to play for people in the hospital. The harp is my healing instrument, and you will be my vessel to bring peace and healing to my people." A huge peace overcame me, but instantly my mind wondered to the thought of *How in the world could I carry a big harp around a hospital?* In His still small voice, once again He said He would provide just what I needed. "Ah okay, Lord," I replied. I had to laugh at myself, though wondering how God would work out all the details. Time would prove once again that He did!

My husband and I loved to travel and go to harp conferences. We decided to go to Lyon & Healy Liturgical Harp Conference, which soon sparked my interest. I attended harp workshops, master classes, and concerts and met some lifelong friends. One special lady we were blessed to meet was named Goodie. Goodie was a very special little red-haired lady well into her late seventies with a spry smile, and everyone adored her! Having a close walk with the Lord, she claimed that God told her that one day she would play the harp. Well, we quickly became friends; and along with another friend, Donna, we all hung out together most of the week at the conference. Goodie did not own a harp yet but knew in her heart that God would provide one for her. She was a woman full of faith and vigor, and her attitude was quite contagious.

A group of us decided we would visit the Lyon & Healy harp factory in Chicago which wasn't too far from Notre Dame, where we were staying. Four of us all piled into the small compact rental car and made our way to the factory for a tour. Lyon & Healy has always been one of the major harp manufacturing businesses in the world, and we were so anxious to see this amazing place where harps were built. Upon entering this one-hundred-year-old building, our eyes watched in amazement at all the varieties of harps made there and the immense skill and time involved in crafting just one harp alone, especially the gold leaf which is applied in an amazingly delicate manner. We all commended that we felt we had truly gone to heaven. What a sight to see!

Even though we saw big beautiful expensive pedal harps in all sizes and finishes, upon leaving, my eyes were instantly drawn to a little lever harp brand-new to their factory. I had never seen a harp so small and yet so lovely. I inquired about it, and they told me she was their newest lap harp. They invited me to play it, and immediately it felt right at home on my lap. What a beautiful tone it had due to the great string tension, and the levers were easy to move. A smile came upon my face as I heard that *still small voice* speak to me, saying, "Verlon, this is the harp you will play in the hospitals." *Oh my,* I thought, *another harp of my own! Well, Lord, if you want me to have this little harp which is easily transportable in a hospital, then so be it.*

Lady Statue Playing Harp (Verlon's home as a child)

CHAPTER 12

It wasn't long till my new little lap harp became a part of my new harp collection. The name Gracie seemed appropriate since she was little and petite. I loved playing her and hearing the delicate sound that sang through her strings. She truly was *the one* best suited for bedside playing and portability.

Thinking about what God told me that quiet evening close to a year ago, I wondered what the next step was to begin playing in the hospitals. Living in the Orlando area, there were many hospitals to choose from, but I had no clue where to begin. Having been a member of our local harp society, I remembered another harpist who played therapeutic harp for one of the downtown hospitals. I contacted Miriam Gentle, and we talked about her work. I told her about how God had spoken to me about playing in the hospitals, and she was very agreeable to help me find my place. She asked if I'd like to come shadow her, and of course, I agreed.

We met at the hospital, and I instantly fell in love with what she did. Playing for the wee babies in the neonatal unit and seeing the positive response was so heartwarming to me. I loved sharing the day with Miriam, and she asked if I would like to meet her boss, of which I was very excited about. I soon met Paula Valleyjo, and we had a wonderful conversation about my heart to minister on the harp for patients. After asking me to play for her, she asked if I'd like to be on staff at Orlando Health. I was ecstatic with excitement! All I could think of was how amazing God had been to open so many doors for me to play my harp. All I knew is that I had found my true calling in life, and I couldn't wait to see what lie ahead in my future.

CHAPTER 13

Becoming a Healing Arts Specialist was an avenue I had never dreamed of as a musician for most of my life. Playing every week for all types of patients in this large hospital was a total new experience for me, and I felt I was doing something that very few people have the opportunity to do. The soothing sounds of the harp in the hallways of the hospital touch not only the patients and staff but also family members. Healing sounds through the harp strings bring a peace everyone needs in this stressful atmosphere. Many times, I would play in the hallways where patients could hear, and people would remark favorably about the healing sounds they experienced and the peace they felt.

Often I would go to specific patients who were experiencing a lot of pain and ask if they would like some therapeutic harp music. Most of the time, patients replied favorably, and I would observe amazing results. Watching the monitors for patients would reveal a slower heartrate, lower blood pressure, and create a calming environment, allowing the patient to drift off to sleep.

When I first began playing in the hospital, I remember playing for a young woman who was drawn up in a fetal position in her bed. The room was dark, and I felt a sense of depression in the room. I began playing some arrhythmic music to match her mood and then moved into more rhythmic music at a slow tempo. I played about twenty minutes in her room, and she suddenly began moving out of her fetal position and began lying in a normal back position and then moved onto her side. She faced me, and I smiled at her and asked if she felt better. She replied with a smile that she did, indeed. The charge nurse came into the room and was amazed how the patient responded so positively. It was then that I witnessed the power of therapeutic harp music!

When I first began playing in the hospital, I would carry appropriate music with me and set it on my music stand. I would pray and ask the Lord what I should play and to guide me by His Spirit. I felt the anointing of God on me as I played, and one time, I experienced a situation that was amazing. The Lord spoke to my heart and clearly told me to put my music away and play what He would lay on my heart. I couldn't believe what I was hearing! He calmly told me to trust Him and play as He led. "Okay, Lord," I said. I can tell you that I did not feel very confident! He then told me to play "Country Road, Take Me Home." I laughed and remembered thinking, *God, that's not a song of hope!* He told me to play it, anyway. Again, I laughed to myself and started playing "Country Road, Take Me Home" in the hallway of the hospital. If you know the song, you know it is happy and upbeat. Well, it wasn't long before a couple came out of a room, approached me, and thanked me for playing that particular song. They then proceeded to tell me that their dad was a patient in the nearby room and was feeling somewhat depressed and they didn't want to leave him alone. Then all of a sudden, when he heard his all-time favorite song, "Country Road," he smiled and felt much better! He knew it was a divine sign from God that he was not alone after all. I was amazed at how I almost missed this special opportunity.

From then on, I never carried my music notebook with me again. The Lord reminded me that I had a storehouse of music inside of me since childhood and that He would pull out what He wanted me to play for each person I met. All I needed to do was trust Him.

"GRACE" Lyon & Healy 17 Semi-Grand

CHAPTER 14

Traveling downtown each week to play therapeutic harp music was a joy which I looked forward to. I never knew what type of experience I would encounter or where I would be led to play. I played in waiting rooms for family members, some of whom had been there for hours and days at a time, depending upon the severity of the patient. My eyes were opened to all the medical staff had to endure from day to day and observing their stress level. Therapeutic harp music was something they were so grateful for because they knew how relaxing the music was and how it helped patients much more effectively.

It wasn't long before I was asked to play for three major hospitals downtown. I played for many different types of patients—those in ICU in critical condition from automobile and motor cycle accidents or those who had fallen off ladders with multiple crushed bones; those in burn units; and of course, oncology patients coming in for their chemo treatments. I played in emergency rooms, for pre-op and post-op surgical patients, as well as recovery rooms. Sometimes after a patient awoke, they thought they had entered heaven when they heard harp music! I encountered everything from sad to funny experiences. Most of all, many sad experiences abounded, and I found myself praying for so many people.

Then there were happy experiences playing for moms in labor to prepare them for childbirth and little preemie babies who were striving to grow. Once I played for seven hours for a mother in labor (of course with rest periods) which helped relax her and bring a healthy baby boy into this world. Heartfelt experiences were numerous, and I felt so blessed to provide a healing atmosphere to everyone involved.

After several years of traveling to the downtown hospitals, I thought about contacting hospitals closer to my home and inquiring about playing for patients and staff. It wasn't long before another door opened for me to be on staff at South Seminole Hospital, which was smaller and much more convenient. I enjoyed playing four hours a week for various types of patients, staff, and families. I grew to love all the staff there, and we looked forward to seeing one another each week. It was a win-win situation for everyone there. Because this hospital was in my neighborhood, I frequently saw many people I knew and was able to touch the lives of so many people through therapeutic harp music. What a blessing!

Doors began to open more and more for opportunities to minister on the harp not only to hurting souls but to a variety of people. I would often be asked to play for weddings or to share my harp testimony at churches. Every day was a new experience, and I never knew what to expect each time I played in the hospitals.

CHAPTER 15

As I began to ponder on the amazing therapeutic effects music had on patients, my mind led me to think of all the different scenarios and places harp music would be beneficial. Playing in the hospitals, I often encountered patients who were dying and knew these people needed a special type of music to ease their suffering.

I decided to contact a local hospice facility to inquire about playing for dying patients. I spoke with a lovely lady who quickly got me involved in going to patients' homes for their end-of-life care. I felt so privileged to be a part of this sacred moment to provide healing harp sounds to not only the patient but also to the family members as well. Once again, each situation was uniquely different, and I observed so much during these years of playing.

The hospice nurse works in palliative care and helps provide means to end-of-life issues such as anxiety and psychological challenges like delirium and depression. A safe quiet environment is provided to help stabilize the patient and provide respite.

I learned that the patient needed different types of music: unfamiliar, arrhythmic with no steady beat. Many times the shades would be drawn, and visitors would leave. It was hard for family to understand that sometimes patients needed to be alone yet needing something like soothing music to ease the patients' pain. This is where bedside therapeutic harp music provides a solace for the hurting soul.

The goal of hospice care is to alleviate emotional and physical symptoms, making time spent at the end-of-life not merely tolerable but very precious. As I played my bedside harp, I observed palliative patients of all ages take their last breath and quietly fall asleep. Many times, I observed patients with sweet smiles on their faces as they breathed their last breath, but occasionally I would play outside the hospital room for a dying patient, and there would be a lot of agitation in the room and turmoil. I quietly played healing soothing music to calm their fears so they could be at peace and then drift off.

Playing for palliative care patients is not easy, but I came to appreciate the precious gift of life we have all been given and the privilege we have to use our gifts to help others in times of need.

"GRACIOUS" Thormahlen Swan Lever Harp

CHAPTER 16

After playing in hospitals for a number of years, being active playing in the harp world, going to conferences and workshops, and reading articles on the amazing therapeutic benefits of harp music, I started thinking about getting more education on the therapeutic benefits of music. I had several colleagues who were also harpists, and we discussed taking the necessary courses to become a Certified Music Practitioner (CMP). There was a lot of talk in the harp world about gaining knowledge in the hows and whys of playing for patients. It wasn't long before my two friends and I decided to register for classes, which meant we had to travel to another city in Florida for a weekend every other month for training.

The education and knowledge I received was invaluable, and I learned so much about all the benefits music holds for patients. Various types of musicians took the course, but many played the harp. The courses were taught by nationally recognized and accredited instructors who taught us all the ins and outs of playing for patients. We soon learned "playing" for patients was *not* "performing." Therapeutic music aids in the healing process and in life and death transitions. We were trained how to serve all types of patients of all ages to create a healing environment for critically ill, chronically ill, disabled, elderly, birthing mothers, children, and dying patients. I learned live therapeutic harp music can reduce blood pressure, alleviate headaches, accelerate physical healing, relieve anxiety and stress, provide a way to release emotions, facilitate the transition from life to death, help with pain management, open the way for grieving, relieve tension, ease the delivery birthing process, and furnish companionship.

The two years of study that included reading many books on therapeutic music helped me gain more than adequate knowledge of the marvelous healing benefits of therapeutic music. Following my studies, I began my forty-five hours of clinical internship at a large local hospital as well as at an Alzheimer's/dementia medical facility.

The experience was invaluable, and I observed patients in a whole new way through all the training I had received. After the many years of being a part of the music world, never would I have believed the amazing benefits that music has on healing. For this, I am so grateful to be a part of something that brings healing to people throughout the world.

CHAPTER 17

Having played the piano since childhood and now playing the harp brought a lifetime of joy and fulfillment to me. I was getting quite comfortable on the harp since starting at middle age, and the music seemed to flow through my fingers with ease. Playing in many hospitals as people entered the building, sitting in waiting rooms and playing for special events the hospitals held, put me in front of a lot of people. People often thought they heard harp music being piped in through the sound system until they saw me visibly. They often remarked what a soothing atmosphere it provided and frequently asked me if I had recorded a CD. I replied no many times until I heard that still small voice tell me that recording a CD was my next assignment.

I questioned the Lord many times stating I had never done anything like that before and furthermore didn't know how! Where do I go? How do I do that? He gently told me He would lead me. Where God assigns, He provides. I said, "Okay," and let it go, trusting that He would put the right people in my path to get the job done.

Well, God certainly has a sense of humor and often does things in unorthodox ways. I needed to see my local jeweler to have my watch repaired, and Chris and I began talking. He asked me how my music was going and was anything new with me. I laughed and stated that God had told me He wanted me to record a harp CD. I explained I didn't have a clue how to do it or where to start. Chris was a fantastic musician himself whom I admired and knew well. Chris began telling me he had a recording studio and would be happy to assist me. "Are you kidding?" I said. "Of course not!" He explained he had recorded many musicians but never a harpist. He was excited to help. I was stunned at how God had led me to him so quickly!

Okay, so the next thing I needed to do was to make a list of songs to record. I told the Lord I needed to know what songs He wanted me to include. I sat quietly with a pad and pen and He gave me the names of twenty songs, some classical and some Christian worship music. He then told me that I was to record my first CD on my therapy harp, Gracie, which had touched so many lives in the health care industry. Also as I prayed over the title of the CD, God led me to Matthew 11:28 and told me to name it *Rest for Your Soul*.

Okay, now I had my song list and recording engineer. Next I needed to know where to get the packaging and duplicating done. I knew a friend who worked for a large music company, and I contacted her and asked if she knew anyone who could provide the services I needed. Immediately, she gave me the name of a guy who was a graphic designer and had tons of knowledge about duplication and packaging CDs. I gave Nate a call, and the next step began. I couldn't believe how easy God had made all of this!

Nate and I met, and we felt a great connection. He had wonderful ideas to share with me, and I became so excited. From then on, everything seemed to fall into place so smoothly, and before I knew it, the actual recording time arrived.

My husband and I met with Chris at his recording studio and discussed the process. I played a trial piece and then listened. Everything sounded clear and clean. Thankfully, it didn't seem overwhelmingly hard to do. Chris looked over my song list and asked if I'd like to start recording right then, so I did. I recorded all twenty songs without having to replay any of them. Chris was amazed, saying that had never happened to anyone he had ever recorded. I was stunned and amazed!

He prepared it for duplication, and within a matter of weeks, my first CD was recorded and packaged. My heart smiled as I looked at it, thinking never in a million years would I have expected to record a harp CD! When deciding on the amount of CDs to purchase, the difference between five hundred and a thousand was quite minimal so by faith, I jumped in and ordered the larger amount. Much to my amazement, when I started selling my CDs, I sold one thousand the first year and had to reorder!

Thanking God for bringing this to pass, He quietly spoke to my heart, saying there would be at least four CDs I would eventually record. Standing in amazement once again, I trusted and knew in my heart that God had a plan and would bring it all to pass. All I needed to do now was simply wait and listen. Within the following two years, my second and third harp CDs were recorded: *Silhouette of Strings* and *Gift for the Giver*.

Music Stand given by Verlon's Dad.

CHAPTER 18

When I first started playing the harp, I attended a harp concert put on by gospel jazz harpist Greg Buchanan, at a church in the Orlando area. I was in awe of this man's talent and how he used it for God's glory. I had only heard classical or pop music played on the harp but never jazz gospel music! He had developed a unique style of playing unlike any other person I'd ever heard. It was amazing to watch him use so many techniques I had never seen before and the constant movement of pedals, which at that time I was unfamiliar with. Above all was his moving testimony that touched so many hearts. One could tell God truly had His hand on this man! When I left the concert, I was truly motivated to keep practicing and develop good harp skills and become the best harpist I could be.

About a year later, I heard about the Lyon & Healy Pop & Jazz Harp Conference in California, and I desperately wanted to attend. The harp presenters looked amazing, and I discovered Greg Buchanan would be one of the presenters. I was so excited to register! This was the first harp conference I had ever attended; and my teacher, Jan Jennings, was also a workshop presenter among many excellent others. I couldn't wait for this new experience and really looked forward to meeting other fellow harpists.

I had a nonstop flight into Los Angeles and then took a smaller plane into the local town where the conference would be held. I remember seeing other people who looked like they were possibly attending the harp conference because they were carrying harp totes. One particular lovely lady I made friends with was Vicki Garcia from Clearwater, Florida. She looked like the perfect model of a harpist with her flowing long blonde hair and sweet manner. We bonded very quickly, and when I discovered she was from Clearwater, I asked her jokingly if she happened to know a good friend of mine named Betsy Kader. She surprisingly responded that she did, saying, "She's one of my very best friends, and we attend church together." Betsy and I had gone to college together and had remained in touch throughout the years. I knew God had amazingly brought Vicki and me together for this trip. In our conversation, I found out we knew many of the same harpists. *Small world*, I thought.

Vicki and I attended Greg Buchanan's workshops, and we had the privilege of eating together with him at mealtimes. What a delight and honor to meet these special people! The guest artists and workshops were all wonderful, opening up a new world of information about the harp, but the most rewarding time was when Greg offered to have an impromptu worship service in the chapel. Many of us bonded there in that holy atmosphere where Christ was lifted up in praise and worship. What an awesome experience.

Being at the conference on oceanfront property suddenly made me feel very cold. It seemed to happen all at once. I remarked to my three roommates that I didn't feel well, and before I knew it, they called 911. I was delirious, shaking uncontrollably, freezing, and taken by ambulance to the local hospital. This was *not* what I bargained for! I still had so many concerts and workshops I wanted to attend. This was not fair!

I was diagnosed with viral pneumonia and was quite ill. Being thousands of miles away from my home in Florida without my husband made me very unhappy! People at the conference heard of my illness, and some came for a short visit. It was so good seeing people I had just met that week who showed they cared. My heart was truly touched. But the most shocking visit I had was that of Greg Buchanan. How special of him to take time out of this conference to visit and pray for me! That was a moment I will forever remember. God revealed His love for me through all these special people, giving me hope and encouragement to get better.

Unfortunately, I missed a number of days attending the harp conference, but I knew it was more important to get well. I had a team of doctors treating me, all which told me I was quite sick and needed to stay put in the hospital. All of my friends were packing up for their trip home, and I certainly didn't want to be alone in a strange town and hospital with no friends or family. I prayed for God's direction, and He reminded me He was taking care of me, so I was directed to check myself out of the hospital and fly home to Florida. After talking with my husband, we both agreed that was the best solution. When I told the doctors to release me so I could travel home, they strongly disagreed, but I relinquished all responsibility of them and flew home. The stewardesses all knew I was quite ill and took good care of me on the five-hour plane trip home, and upon arriving at the airport terminal, a wheelchair and my husband were waiting for me. What a joy to finally be back on familiar ground. In the weeks thereafter, I went to a specialist who told me to stay home for about a month and get well. That I did! I was, indeed, thankful that God took such good care of me and that He put the right people at the right time in my path to help navigate my path to wellness.

CHAPTER 19

Many times when I played at the hospitals, I would meet interesting new people. Once when playing my bedside harp for a patient, he spoke of his daughter who had wanted to learn to play the harp for quite a while. It wasn't long before his daughter phoned me to discuss harp lessons. Bonnie began taking lessons soon after.

Bonnie told me that her husband wrote a column for a local newspaper, and before I knew it, he phoned me and wanted to schedule an interview with me on playing therapeutic harp music in the hospitals. Gary was a nice gentleman and invited me to talk with him over lunch. I agree to meet him, and we enjoyed talking about all the different experiences I had encountered while playing for patients in the hospitals. He wrote his article, and it was circulated locally and then throughout the country. It wasn't long before I was contacted by another journalist who wanted to write an article on me sharing the benefits of therapeutic harp music also. I met her as well, and soon more articles were circulated throughout the country. Before I knew it, I was getting e-mails from people around the country who were interested in doing what I was doing. Word spread rapidly, and I stood in amazement!

The more I played in the hospitals, the more opportunities I was given to meet people who asked if I played for weddings. Many people seeing the harp dream of having a harpist play for their wedding, and such was the case for nurses. Soon I was asked to play for many weddings and parties through the people I met at the hospital. In addition, I would meet pastors who invited me to share my harp testimony and play for their church. More and more doors opened, and I was definitely not lacking for great harp experiences!

CHAPTER 20

There was a very dear lady God brought into my life in the year 2000. She moved to Orlando from West Palm Beach and was introduced to me by a friend. Joy Aber was a jewel and a mighty prayer warrior. She never had any children of her own but always wanted them, especially a daughter. I was quickly "adopted" by her, and she became my "adopted" mom. We prayed for one another a lot, and she became a regular part of our family.

One particular day, she told me the Lord told her that I was supposed to teach the harp. I laughed and asked her if she had heard correctly. She was quiet, and as time went on, she made the same remark. One day after taking her home, driving down the street, I sensed a strong voice telling me to take my business cards to a nearby tea room. I wondered if I was just hearing voices. Ha! The impression came again quite strongly, and I soon obeyed. I entered the tea room and asked the proprietor if I could leave my business cards. She fondly agreed.

Just a few days later, I received a phone call from a lady who told me she was on the board of St. Andrews Church and Music Conservatory. She commented that she had gone to a luncheon at the exact tea room I had left my business cards at and wanted to speak with me about teaching harp lessons at their conservatory. I knew this was another God incidence for sure! Immediately, I remembered the strong impression I had about leaving my business cards at that very tea room. The lady told me the board had been praying for a harp instructor for some time. We discussed my Christian faith, and she strongly felt she was led to me. She told me someone from the conservatory would contact me soon to set up an interview, which happened soon after.

Seeing the church and conservatory led me to believe that the students enrolled there were serious music students. Randal Van Megglan, dean of the conservatory, along with another board member, greeted me as I entered. They talked about the great appreciation they had for quality classical and sacred music. Upon asking what experience I had, I shared how the Lord had led me to the harp in my adult life and that I had a music degree with over twenty-five years of experience in teaching and performing. Feeling very comfortable with the interview, I knew God had, indeed, opened this door to be their first harp instructor.

When God calls you to do something, He always provides for your every need. I held a meeting with interested members of the church and those in the nearby areas to talk about learning to play the harp. A nice crowd attended, and before I knew it, I had a good amount of first time harp students. In the weeks that followed, I collected as much information as I could about beginning group harp lessons, and a new chapter of my life began. I taught not only harp there but also piano lessons. I had students of all ages and enjoyed teaching the very thing that brought new life to me. My students played regularly for recitals and Federation, and one student even decided to study harp in college. The joy that came from teaching there was wonderful, and I felt tremendously blessed to have the opportunity to inspire students in this amazing instrument that we all loved so much.

Before long, my teaching studio began growing by leaps and bounds with more people interested in harp lessons. When people realized that I had begun playing the harp as an adult, it gave them encouragement to begin playing the harp themselves. God showed me that whatever dream you may have, when God is in it, age is never a barrier. To this day, teaching has been my passion, and the best part of all is being able to see how this incredible instrument changes lives, not only the one playing the harp but the listener as well.

CHAPTER 21

Joy, my friend I shared about earlier, was like a second mom to me after my own mother had passed away. Even though she was much older than me, we found we had so much in common. She loved the arts and had even authored a book of poetry which was quite anointed by the Lord. We talked often about recording a CD with her speaking poetry as I played soothing harp music in the background.

Joy really had no family to speak of, only a stepson and grandchildren from his side of the family who made no time to include Joy in their family gatherings. Yet when she was invited for a holiday outing, she was left alone with no one to talk with. Therefore, Joy told me often how special I was to her since our family included her in many of our special occasions. A lot of time was spent with this special lady, and I gleaned a lot of wisdom from her in her old age. God must have known I needed that kind of mentorship in my life.

Joy's health was not the best. She was tall and thin and tried to take care of herself by eating well and exercising her mind and body regularly, but she had heart problems that had lingered with her for most of her adult life. This dear lady, who was not rich by worldly means, was surely rich in God and freely shared her faith with everyone she came in contact with.

After I had been on staff as a healing artist at South Seminole Hospital for a number of years, I received a call telling me that Joy had been admitted for heart issues. She stayed in the hospital for several weeks when the doctors realized she had multiple health problems. Upon hearing of her hospitalization, I went regularly to check on her. It was also quite convenient since I was on staff there that I could play therapeutic harp music for her. It was very healing for her, and we both loved having this special time together.

On one of my regular days to play at the hospital, I went to check on Joy. The doctors seemed to be quite disturbed about her condition, and multiple doctors and nurses surrounded her bed. They told me she could not have visitors at that time. Being very upset, I began praying. In my spirit, I knew this could be the end of Joy's life. She surely loved Jesus and told me a number of times she was ready to meet her Lord. I played my harp outside her room and felt the presence of angels all around. Doctors began to exit her room, and I asked if I could go in. They knew how close Joy and I were and told me it was permissible. I went in and told Joy how much I loved her and the immense love God had for her. She smiled sweetly and, soon closing her eyes, slipped away to heaven. There was a peace that transcended nothing I had ever experienced, and I knew she was seeing the face of her Lord Jesus Christ and was finally home at last.

The days that followed Joy's homecoming were lonely ones for me and some of her close friends. We gave her a Celebration of Life service that compared to none other I had ever attended. Joy had been my mentor and close friend for ten years, and I knew my life was much richer for having known such a beautiful lady.

Chapter 22

Being a therapeutic harpist brought countless blessings I never would have imagined. The variety of patients I saw weekly was an experience unlike any other day. I came to know many staff members by name and looked forward to seeing familiar faces each week. Most of the time I had a set schedule of what hospital I would play at each week, but one particular day, I decided to change going to South Seminole Hospital to a Thursday instead of Tuesday.

I played in various locations in the hospital and then decided to play for the oncology patients while they were taking their chemo treatments. With lunchtime approaching, I took a break to go to lunch. Within minutes, I had a stomachache that came almost instantly. I dropped off my harp at the administration office and quickly exited to the ladies' room where I sat for what seemed like a long time. Then immediately I developed a migraine headache that felt like my brains were exploding followed swiftly by a strong pounding in my chest. I prayed asking God to heal me. After about twenty minutes, I was able to walk into the administration office and sit down. Noticing a change in my demeanor, Kathy asked what was wrong. After resting for a short while in the office, she decided to call the emergency room for someone to check on me. My vitals were taken, and soon I was swiftly scooted to the ER.

I had never experienced such a sick feeling like that before, but the Lord reminded me that He had ordained me to play in the hospital *that particular day* so I could get the necessary help I needed. If I had been at home, I would not have had the instantaneous help I received.

Soon after arriving in the ER, Dr. Arora, who was my assigned cardiologist, arrived. Tests were run immediately, and he told me I had suffered a heart attack. *Oh my goodness*, I thought! Never would

I have imagined that since I had always been healthy and took good care of myself.

My husband and sons were contacted and came soon after. Pastor Hardy came to the hospital immediately after he got the news. I was surrounded by wonderful health care professionals and people I loved. It was during this experience that God revealed His deep love and care for me.

I stayed overnight at South Seminole and taken by ambulance the next morning to the downtown Orlando Health Hospital with an excellent cardiology department. Dr. Arora performed heart catherization surgery and a stent was inserted. After recuperating in the hospital for a number of days, I was then released to go home. God had certainly given me a wake-up call and reminded me that I needed a lot of rest and time to slow down and take better care of myself.

Up to then, my life had always been quite full with teaching and playing in five different hospitals as well as harp gigs like weddings and other events. I had been on staff at these hospitals for a decade, and God reminded me that this was my time to rest.

One month later, my supervisor called one Tuesday morning and asked if I had plans to come play bedside music that day, and I replied, "Of course!" She then told me that the hospitals were discontinuing the Healing Arts Program and this would be my last day. I couldn't believe what I was hearing! This was a ministry dear to my heart and a passion I had enjoyed for over ten years, and it was now coming to an end.

Thinking back over all the wonderful experiences I had ministering to so many people gave me a tremendous feeling of gratitude. Never would I have imagined that God would use music in my life as a healing tool to help others. When the Lord brought me to the harp, I knew exciting new things were in store for my future, but I had no idea the impact it would have upon my life as well as others.

CHAPTER 23

"He has made everything beautiful in its time"
(Ecclesiastes 3:11).

"Delight yourself in the Lord and He will give
you the desires of your heart"
(Psalm 37:4).

Since I first began playing the harp, God has led me to many
other professional harpists whom I've had the pleasure of studying
with. The harp is one of those amazing instruments that you can continue to learn about throughout your life. Every instructor is unique
and has different ideas to impart to the student. For a number of
years, I've enjoyed studying with Mary Bridget Roman, harp professor
at FSU. Even though I'm an adult, I will continue to study and learn
as long as I'm alive. The deep desire to learn this special instrument
will continue to stay with me throughout my time on earth.

In the years that have followed, I've been blessed to minister in
many churches sharing my testimony of God's amazing grace through
playing the harp and seeing the lives He has touched through my
music. He has opened many more doors that I never would have
imagined and taken me on a journey I will never forget. Some of the
additional blessings I have been given besides playing for countless
weddings, funerals, parties, corporate events are teaching workshops
at harp conferences around the country telling about the benefits of
therapeutic harp music among other topics.

The one blessing I enjoy today is playing in my home church
at Casselberry Community, where our music is alive with vibrant
praise and worship. This is where my heart is and will forever be—

playing for my Lord who blessed me with the ability to "Praise the Lord on the Harp" (Psalm 33:2).

I never before realized that music itself could be anointed by God's Spirit to minister to people's heart. That was the beginning of a new power that flows through my music today.

Ever since this journey began for me in 1993, I have been blessed with countless opportunities only God could provide. Indeed, He took a very painful circumstance and used it for my good. My passion was born out of my pain, and for that, I will be forever grateful. Just as the familiar song goes, "Something beautiful, something good, all my confusion, He understood. All I had to offer Him was brokenness and strife, but He made something beautiful of my life" (Bill and Gloria Gaither).

When the Lord told me to write my story a number of years ago, He told me I was to share it with you. You see, this story is not just about *me* but rather about what our mighty God can do through *any* life. God brought the harp into my life as a vehicle to be a healer for the heart and to bring comfort to people. God cares about every soul, and what He did for me, He can do for *you*. He desires to do great things in your life too! Whatever gift or talent he has given you, I encourage you to surrender it completely to Him, and watch what amazing things He will do!

PART 2

STUDY GUIDE
A Harp Named Grace:
An Amazing Journey

This study guide is designed for both personal and group use. It is recommended to read the book in its entirety first for a clear overview of the story and then revisit each chapter as you make your way through the study guide. Or if you prefer, you may take one chapter at a time, reading a chapter, then consider the questions provided for that chapter. You may find it helpful to record your responses and reflections in a journal or notebook. When using the book in a group, you may choose one or two chapters each week. Whichever way you choose, I hope you enjoy reflecting on your own personal adventure and that it leads you closer to the Lord and His will for your life.

Study Guide
A Harp Named Grace

Chapter 1

1. Do you recall a time in your childhood that a seed was planted in you that came to pass later in your life? If so, share with your group what it was and how it impacted your life.
2. Do you have a talent that someone helped you discover? If so, what is your talent, and how do you use it to bless others?
3. Have you ever known someone whose talent inspired you? If so, please share with your group.
4. Did you ever doubt that you could fulfill a dream? Did your dream ever come true? If so, share with your group.
5. Read Matthew 2:11. What treasure could you present to Jesus? Do you think He would be pleased? Is giving your talent or gift a form of worship?
6. Read Matthew 6:19–21. How does this scripture apply to your treasure?
7. Read Matthew 19:16–21. What treasure did the rich young ruler not want to give up? Are you willing to give your gift/treasure to God for His glory? Why or why not?
8. Read Psalm 9:1. Have you ever given thanks to the Lord for giving you your gifts? Do so by writing a prayer of thanksgiving to Him.

Chapter 2

1. Read Ecclesiastes 3:1. What do you think the scripture means? Do you think God has the perfect "season" when our gift will make the biggest impact on our lives as well as others? Explain.
2. Have you expanded your talent by studying and enlarging your knowledge? How, and what did you do?
3. Have you ever experienced burnout or a dimming light when doing something you felt God wanted you to do? If so, how did you deal with it? What did you do to reignite the original fire?
4. Has anything ever happened to you that changed the direction you were originally on? If so, what changed? How did you handle it?
5. Looking back, can you see God's *hand* upon your situation? How did you feel at the time? What encouragement could you give someone today that is walking in a similar situation?

Chapter 3

1. Whom have you had the pleasure to know and love in a special way? How have they impacted your life?
2. Has the Holy Spirit ever prompted you to do something that you were glad you listened and obeyed? Explain the situation and the outcome.
3. Have you ever been in the presence of someone who was dying? How did you feel and handle your sorrow or pain?
4. What do you think Jesus would say to you when you're going through pain? What scriptures come to mind that you could share to help you or someone else feel comforted during the grieving process?

Chapter 4

1. We have all made decisions we later regretted. Think of one that you could openly share with your group.
2. What tragic or unexpected incident have you ever experienced that dramatically impacted your life? Share the feelings you experienced.

Chapter 5

1. When you've lost someone you dearly loved, in what ways were you able to cope? Did others reach out to you during your grieving? How did their presence help you?
2. We've all lost someone we loved. How have you reached out to another person who has lost someone they were very close with? Share with your group some tangible ways you were there to encourage and offer support during difficult times.
3. Has anyone you've known said anything that almost seemed "prophetic" and at a later time the Lord reminded you of those spoken words? What kind of impact did that make upon your life?
4. Who were some of the "ministering angels" who have been there for you when you were grieving or going through a difficult time? What did they do to help bring you comfort?
5. Have you personally ever been a "ministering angel" for someone? In what ways did you minister to them?
6. What scripture(s) can you recall where Jesus was ministered to by angels? (See Matthew 4:11 for starters.)

Chapter 6

1. We have all been through tough times where we've asked God, "Why did this happen!" Share with your group something you experienced that made you ask the same question. How did God bring comfort to you during this time?
2. Do you think anger is a sin? Talk with your group about how God wants us to constructively use anger in a positive way that will lead us on to a healing path.
3. In what ways do you think God uses painful experiences to speak to us?
4. What scriptures can you think of that have helped you when you've felt you were drowning in sorrow?
5. Read Isaiah 43:2, and explain what this scripture means to you.
6. Read Romans 8:28. How has God revealed this promise personally to you?
7. Have you ever felt so depressed that you felt there was no hope? If so, how did God help you through this painful time?
8. Read Jeremiah 29:11. How does this scripture encourage you?
9. Read Psalm 40:3. What does the psalmist mean when he says, "God put a new song in my mouth, a song of praise to our God"? Have you ever felt God gave you a new song after going through a difficult time? Explain.

Chapter 7

1. Have you ever been asked a question that you ended up saying words you never expected to speak and wondered why you spoke those particular words when later you realized the words came directly from God? Share with your group.
2. Has God ever spoken to you personally about a dream you always had? How did you know it was God speaking, and how did it make you feel?
3. Have you ever been given a gift that you always dreamed of having? How did you feel when you received the gift?

4. Is there a gift you long to have now but don't know how God could make it possible for you to own it? If so, share with your group your longtime dream.

5. Do you think God wants you to have your dream fulfilled? If so, why and how would He want you to respond?

6. Have you ever been given a gift that changed your life? (Note that the "gift" doesn't have to be a material one.) Have you seen the "gift" as coming from the *hand* of God? How did it make you feel when you received it?

Chapter 8

1. Have you ever attempted to do or learn something and then later realized you couldn't do it on your own? Share with your group about your experience.

2. What did you do to solve your problem? Read Philippians 4:6.

3. In what ways do you think God has a sense of humor?

4. Has God ever led you to "someone unlikely" that turned out to be an answer to prayer? Explain.

Chapter 9

1. Have you ever embarked upon learning something that you thought was probably easy but you later realized it was difficult? What kind of attitude did you have? Share with your group.

2. Have you ever received a gift from someone that you mysteriously *knew* was really from the Lord?

3. Read Psalm 21:2 and Psalm 37:4. Share with your group what "desires of your heart" you have had and whether you received it.

4. Has God ever given you something that eventually was a healing tool in your life? Share what that gift was and how it brought healing to your heart.

Chapter 10

1. Have you ever desired owning something that seemed completely out of your financial reach? What did you do? Did you ever receive the item, and if so, how did it come to pass?
2. Read Psalm 145:9, 16, and 19. Share with your group the meaning of these scriptures.
3. Read Matthew 7:5, and discuss how this scripture can apply to your heart's desire.
4. What do the words *amazing grace* mean to you? In what ways have you experienced His amazing grace?
5. Have you ever received a financial miracle? Share with your group what happened.
6. Do you believe in coincidences or God incidences? Explain.

Chapter 11

1. Have you ever looked forward to something and God ended up changing the events to open a new way for Him to do something new in your life? If so, describe the situation.
2. Has God ever spoken a message to you that you clearly knew it was His still small voice? What did He say, and how did you feel?
3. Have you ever wondered how God could provide something special to you and later you were the recipient of that gift?
4. Have you ever met someone special whom God put in your path who demonstrated amazing faith? If so, how did that person effect or influence you?
5. Ponder on Habakkuk 2:3. How would you apply it to your heart's desire?

Chapter 12

1. What doors have been opened for you that you knew came directly from God's hand? Share with your group.

Chapter 13

1. Do you have a talent or gift that you have used in a variety of ways? If so, describe your experience, and share how it changed your total perspective of your gift.
2. In what ways have your gift affected others in a positive way?
3. Has God ever told you to do something that you definitely did not feel confident about doing? If so, describe your situation and outcome.
4. Do you believe God has a sense of humor? Has He ever told you to do something that to you did not make sense? If so, share your experience.

Chapter 14

1. In what ways has God opened new doors for you to share your gift with others? What was your experience?

Chapter 15

1. Have you ever had the opportunity to use your gift to minister to someone that was actively dying? Share your experience. Did your sharing bring hope and encouragement to that person?

Chapter 16

1. Have you ever taken your talent to the next level and embarked on a new adventure to stretch your knowledge? If so, share with your group your experience.
2. Referring to question 1, describe the new knowledge you gained and how it changed your perspective.
3. In what ways do you think using our talents blesses other people?

Chapter 17

1. Has God ever told you to do something you thought you could never successfully do? What was it, and describe the outcome?
2. Explain the meaning of the phrase: "Where God assigns, He provides." Then read Proverbs 3:5–6, and share with your group.
3. Read Romans 11:33–36, and share how you think God can use your gift for His *glory*.
4. Has God ever given you a specific scripture that instantly spoke to you? If so, what scripture was it, and how did it impact you?
5. Read Ephesians 3:20, and share what this means to you.

Chapter 18

1. Have you ever been on a traveling adventure where God put a special person in your life for that particular trip? If so, share your story with your group.
2. If you are a believer in Christ, many times it's easy to sense another fellow Christian God may put in your path. In what ways can you tell?
3. Have you ever had a terrible experience where your world was shaken in an unusual way? If so, share your experience with your group.
4. Did you have a special "someone" who prayed for you and ministered to you through that period of time?
5. Read 1 Peter 5:7, and share how that scripture has ministered to you personally.

Chapter 19

1. Have you ever had a new door open for you, and before you knew it, it had spread like wildfire? If so, share with your group.
2. How do you think that experience impacted other people?

Chapter 20

1. Have you ever had a special friend God introduced you to that ended up being a part of your family? If so, who was it, and how did that person impact your life?
2. Have you ever felt a strong impression to do something and later realized it was God speaking to your heart? Share your experience with your group.
3. Read Acts 6:25–31, and describe Phillip's experience in how he was led to the Ethiopian eunuch.
4. Has God ever opened a new door to you that you felt was led by the Holy Spirit? If so, describe your experience.
5. Have you ever felt "called" by the Lord to minister in some way to others? If so, please share your ministry calling.
6. What is your *dream*? Have you ever stepped out and pursued it? Do you think your dream is limited by your age? Why or why not?
7. Read Psalm 21:2–4, and describe how this verse fits with your dream.

Chapter 21

1. Have you ever had a mentor in your life that encouraged you a lot in your Christian walk? If so, share your experiences.
2. Who do you know that is a wise woman? What do you think makes her so wise?
3. In your opinion, what makes a person rich? Read Proverbs 22:1. Share other scriptures that support your views.
4. Read Proverbs 17:17a and 18:24. Share with your group what makes a good friend.

Chapter 22

1. Has God ever changed *your* schedule for a certain reason and later you realized *His* plan was definitely more important? If so, share your experience with your group.
2. Have you ever been through a tough time when the Lord revealed His great love for you? If so, please share with your group.
3. Is your life full of activities that if God spoke to you right now, He would say it's time to stop some of these and slow down? If you are in that position now or have been, please share with your group the importance of taking care of ourselves and resting.
4. Has a door ever been closed to you that you hated to see closed but realized it was God's will for that time in your life? If so, share your experience.
5. Have you thanked God for the wonderful ways He has blessed you by sharing your gift with others. If you haven't, tell Him now how grateful you are.

Chapter 23

1. Read Ecclesiastes 3:1 and 11. Do you believe God has a plan for your life? What do you think He wants to do with it, and how do you think He wants you to respond?
2. Read Philippians 4:13. In what ways do you think God can use painful circumstances and use them for our good?
3. Sometimes, we learn that a new passion is born out of pain. Has that ever happened to you? If so, would you share with your group?
4. Do you believe God can take our brokenness and use it for good to bring others closer to Him?
5. God is no respecter of persons. What He did for me, He can do for *you* too. He desires to accomplish great things through you for His glory. He wants to use *you* to touch other people's lives. What are you willing to completely surrender to

Him right now? I encourage you to lift your "gift or talent" up to the Lord and see what amazing things He will do for you! In the below space, write out your prayer of commitment, and thank Him for blessing you with your gift.

Philippians 1:6 says, "For I am confident of this very thing, that He who began a good work in you will perfect it until the day of Christ Jesus."

Closing Quotes

Life is a precious gift from God. Don't waste it. Live life to the fullest! Live with passion!

What would you attempt to do if you knew you could not fail?

Don't be afraid to dream. Imagine what you are capable of, and live that life. Life is not over until you breathe your last breath.

Some people walk the path of their youth and give up; now in their old age, they believe it's too late for them to seek their dream. Never stop seeking!

Live the life you've imagined.

Go and let your life shine!

(Some of the above quotes came from *The Rhythm of Life: Living Every Day with Passion and Purpose* by Matthew Kelly.)

Verlon with "GRACE" harp